BIG MEDICINE COMES TO ERIE

The Black Moss Press First Lines Poetry series is for writers who are publishing their first book of poetry.

Books in the First Lines series include:

Big Medicine
Comes to Erie

by D.A. Lockhart

Black Moss
Press
2016

FIRST EDITION

Library and Archives Canada Cataloguing in Publication

Lockhart, D. A., 1976-, author
    Big medicine comes to Erie / D.A. Lockhart.

(First lines poetry)
Poems.
ISBN 978-0-88753-564-2 (paperback)

    I. Title. II. Series: First lines poetry

PS8623.O295B53 2016   C811'.6   C2016-903762-2

Cover photo: Native American Basket, by Bruce - user name Stockton350, found on Creative Commons and licensed at https://creativecommons.org/licenses/by/2.0/legalcode

Editing: Alicia Labbé
Design: Karen Veryle Monck

 Black Moss
Press
www.blackmosspress.com

Published by Black Moss Press
2450 Byng Road
Windsor, ON N8W 3E8 Canada

Black Moss books are distributed in Canada and the U.S. by Fitzhenry & Whiteside. All orders should be directed there.

Black Moss Press acknowledges the support of the Canada Council for the Arts and the Ontario Arts Council for its publishing program.

 ONTARIO ARTS COUNCIL
CONSEIL DES ARTS DE L'ONTARIO

 Canada Council   Conseil des Arts
for the Arts   du Canada

PRINTED IN CANADA

For Emily

Contents

The Time Before

The World as We Have Inherited

The Time Before

Barometric Pressure

Always start with poems about places
that sing themselves as if they were a whir
of mid-august heat bugs. Begin each
with words by other people, famous
or should be famous, stoically preserved.
Start them with the things others say
about the curvature that lives must follow
so as to say we are not alone in our time
and these moments all now belong as much
to them as they do to us. Colonel Talbot
and Tecumseh and Hiriam Walker rising
and falling and casting long shadows
upon the prairies and cleared forest. Speak
those words in the only voice given,
one-in-the-same as the crack of ice
against the shore, deep horns calling fog
in the distance, fishflies popping under
foot, and the descent of jetliners across
the border that separates treaty-makers
from those that straddle the boundaries
of their inheritance. Repeat it all
because to be alone is to have only land,
and memories of soil and rock are measured
by the passage of cold and warm fronts.

Gamwig Predicts the Arrival

In the space between the world
tree and the eastern fire
of this big house, the vision
comes like waves dragging
foam inland from the sea.
Each arrival meaning others
must move, becomes froth
dominates and displaces that
which it contacts. A vision
that reminds us all medicine
can turn bad, scared turn
to lost, and what we see
rarely weakens its arrival.

Brought to life by the passing
of another season, our sacred
space aglow with fire that no
narrative could extinguish, our future
to be carved with shaking bones,
shooting stars, and the manner
migration shapes us to lands
we will know only in passing.

It is simple: The foam will come
ashore. The vision brought
from the waning light between
posts of our big house and stories
of tragedies that curiosity begins,
about those foreign to ceremonial
fires and the paths that people must
walk due to the arrival of others.

And so the Prophet Speaks the World into Existence

From the sycamore forest line
the world as we know it
comes as a thought turning
from vision to speech atop
the thickness of tree frogs
singing before a thunderstorm,
the syllables of Tippecanoe
before being named itself,
and the quiet of corn fields
in the anxiety of wind.

Spoke into being, a confederacy
fueled by shooting stars
and movement of quiet ground.
A migration to come, spurred
on by unending massacres
and the supremacy of religions
too young to know of potlaching
and the mixed-blood nature
of existence. As Harrison's men
smudge the people from their
land, the shooting star persists,
moves to north. In its wake, us.
What follows is necessity, the pomp
and thunder by which we escape
from promise cut short several lines
from the end it refuses to meet.

Neolin Liberates Detroit

At crucifixion, Europeans had killed
their own gods. Crosses carried across
oceans to Turtle Island were to remind
of the powers they believed they had
to seize upon the path of righteousness.
The power of conquest lies in self-belief.

Neolin stands in the timberline outside
the walls of Fort Detroit. Proclaiming
the river narrows free from the dominion
of surveyors and the soothsayers of beliefs
birthed in the uprising of the profane
against that which once was sacred.

His speech comes heavier than westerlies
and the fury with which they can bring the sky
down with. Words enough to shake the deer
and beaver and sturgeon from the land.
For that which sustains us cannot sustain
those which would kill their own prophets
or sacrifice what is divine. He leaves as quiet

as he arrives. Confederacies and war parties follow
in his wake and do little to the fortress walls
or the men that will one day ignore them.
Uprisings and war clatter are best left
to acts of desperation that begin and end
with disbelief in the way our world is
in every way an act of the divine.

Wenebest Ascends the Shoreline
North of the Maumee River

Witness as he arrives
from the shallows
of nearly still water near shore,
arising as if from baptism
afforded to newcomers.

Know that he is atavistic
as the rivers themselves,
that meet in his wake.
Night broke open
by water fowl fleeing
skyward from the shore,
away from hiding,
past the hushed gait
of men at war.

The land before him quiet
like in a silence that precedes
men in a late autumn hunt.

The creatures we must align with
are measured only by the degrees
of victories held by surviving stories
and the whims of passing storms.

He moves inland
towards an earth
that will know blood
by his hands
and those of his men.
Surefooted they stalk
the ghosts of a past
collective in the ways

they've retreated
from the advance
of a violence
not of their making.

From Crafty One
to Crippled Hand,
and prophetic vision
to agitated drunk,
the battles before him
will bear him a name
that speaks to weakness
and not to the fear
they have placed in him.

In this night,
the confederacy must stand
the watershed a birthright,
and water runs-off cold
from warm-weathered bodies
into a slow-exhaled night.

What follows, before
the tales of nation building
and the demise of savage
prairies is anger,
coaxed like heat
from coals white-hot
in the dew-heavy bleakness
of a cold autumn morning
stirred from memories
of homes burned
in the wake of land settlements
and a hunger set ablaze,
one which can belong
to no man.

Big Medicine comes to the Shores of Erie

Fire, swung above,
gouges the darkness
left by moon set.
Slow embers are shed
into cool humid air.

The shore rises
in anticipation of light.
This dance, decisive,
leads hide-covered feet
as they meet sand and grass
and misplaced stones.

Between inland seas,
the earth is pushed up
by the exhalation of turtles.
Steady in the rise and fall
of fire coaxing wind to course
back to life, water pushes
to flow far and strong.

Waters recede.
Manitou break the surface,
rise to greet
this fresh movement
of fire and flesh.

Perspective of Generations
Beneath this Great Lakes Clipper

Across borders drawn in waves
restless as tall grass prairies, visions
emerge from shore of gunpowder
bottomed storms cutting crooked
against cornflower pastel skies.

That nickel gray lake below churns
despite treaties cut into air and
sealed with sacred rituals, churns
with distant rumbles like war
on the frontier the better part
of a lifetime across the shallow lake.

Gathered against the lake's edge,
wind biting into the harden clay
of our skin, we listen so to understand
distant movements, hoping frontiers
are places where myths return from
and not the land we stand upon.
It comes with a hope that our
footholds begin new stories
that will stand the winds and rains
of every storm that will follow.

As if coaxed on by white cap teeth
the four-masted great lakes clipper
moves off to the east, fleeing
some skirmish it cannot win.
Still the relentless waves gouge
at the shore line we stand upon,
and we know that in the perspective
of generations before us, every four

masted storm upon these waters
should remind us that life
itself comes from a series
of near landfalls and the flight
from those we were certain slipped
past us in the time before sunset.

Jackson Park Grandstand
in the Waning Light of 1957

As fire gives way to ash
and the world that belongs
to us comes to greet sunset,
yellow, sideways light reminiscent
of Easter morning on daffodils,
sundresses, and tender lawns,
we must speak of resurrections
and the routes one takes north.

Now with that red light surge
against shadow and the low-slung
defeat in the firemen shoulders
as they move off into this night
the world should know that it will
not be the same as we knew before.

So begins the second gospel
of Emancipation and into the quiet
felt by those that have come to call
the place where ember and ash
have turned pomp and jubilation
into the basic act of getting by
in a place that has welcomed fire
as the element that binds us all
to the footprints we have fled to.

Silence Follows Sebakwat

Did it begin with the sebakwat
of trees and brush in rising fury
cast by clouds as they pushed
past? Was it like a brittle talon
down the spine, leaving the hair
to stand up on the back of the neck,
perception of the space around them
caught in straight-up twitch? Raw
animal sense that the earth
was to be shoveled back by the sky.

Did the elm, the ash, the oak
give way and snap, rising
to circulate with the air
as if the atmosphere itself grew
violent and immovable
all at once as if it were a roadway
taken at speed, water finding
its way back to the bottom.

What followed had to be the clearing,
the wide open sky and gravity driven cascade
of loose leaves, tumbling as if pushed
by a single steady breath back to earth.
And lying there, underside resting on damp
ground, they were softly warmed by sun.

We know that silence followed. And gasps
of those missed by the violence, those
that came within a certain clearance
of the sweet hereafter, garrisoned
between concessions and shielded
from the deluge of earth and tree limbs

and the detritus of gimcrack shelters,
echoed the flutter of starlings roosting
on the twisted grandstands and utility poles
that lay crooked to sky they once dominated.

Ensuing reports from Toronto avowed
the twister came from Rouge River,
followed Turkey Creek, and took with it
fourteen people before unleashing
a rash of stolen lawnmowers and reducing
the race-track to a future history lesson.
Leaving a nagging sense that bad weather
comes from the west and follows water.

Ghosts of Tecumseh

Through outstretch and fading waves
of vibrato sound and burning musk
as it fills raven humid air, hovering,
almost visibly in the night, we walk
and are wrapped in the orange and steel
of light posts, glow thrown down in
electric hum, and us suspended lazily
grow numb, soaked by car plant machinery.

Concession to concession, this night
is ours. With lots of blueprint houses
burning their brick-base settler dream
into the land Tecumseh died for. We,
footnotes taken from long-form censuses,
struggle with the ghosts of those places
and prophets that deposited us here. Each
of us born into this world knowing
that they always amp up the worst things
when the world sleeps between shifts.
Along these river narrows once driven
by tides and fast moving weather fronts,
quiet follows passing cars and trucks. Now,
the belief is to work away the places we've been
in the last few spaces where people come to change
labour and time into profit. This night should be
ours. Instead, it falls to the rhythm and haze
of a July night in a city quick to forget
that which came before and us walking
eastward down a road named for a martyr
that all too few are willing to recall.

Wejack Embarks from the West above Lake Erie

Wejack embarks above the horizon,
from the home of waters and edge
of the sky. Wejack moves through
as if on the soft ground of freshly shed
leaves in the dampness before snow.

The night leaks out from the east
and fades into the distant lights
of factories, subdivisions, power plants.
Above them Wejack rises coyly
to meet the leading edge of darkness.

Beneath igniting stars, the last freighters
of the season burn on towards the ocean
past breakers, babbling gulls, sandbars.
Wejack chases them from the land,
steady as in the certain arrival of night.

In that great reflective slick of heaven,
the distant deck lights burn in a panic
as ocean-bound freighters flee the cold
the Fisher brings, with unsaid knowledge
that the stubborn stalking winds come
when the afterlife brushes against things
they left behind and they still crave.

Perfect Proportions of the River of Souls

To be sure our prophets came
to us during the night,
warning of erosion
speaking steady
like silt flowing downstream.
Visions of land turned
and the world consumed
in floods that no skeleton dance
could turn back.

Stretched above, wide
and bright, the river of souls
cascaded from horizon
to horizon in perfect proportions.
Itself a prophet, bent in
closer to us, as if the past
would descend upon
those it left behind.

Because the coast
was two generations away,
the Moravians still close,
and the prophets had
wrapped the bones.

In proportion, we knew we must move

again.

The World as We Have Inherited

Coming to the Mission to the Hurons

You've come to this place
at the base of a bent line road
that ascends a river
and falls away
into a nation
beyond the straits.

The Assumption Church,
once the second Mission
to the Hurons,
rises alongside
into tarnished copper
spires and burnt coke
turrets.

Divinity made concrete
and pushed crooked
by the even descent
of time.

Indifferent trucks climb
above the orange and yellow
of the fall canopy that hides
the absence of Huron villages;
the smoke and longhouses
and beached canoes that followed
the once aligned forms
of the mission.

People the French had named
for the wild boar
then chased away
into the slow sprawl of farmland

by the hard metallic lines
that conceived of this bridge
and those modern pack animals
that now snort their mechanical grunts
in their ascent of the rusted teal
and metal cables spreading out above

Pointe De Montreal, and together
those that left here list
with the rows of empty houses
and quiet of city streets.
All dwarfed beneath
the adjacent towers of the mission,
and the feel of glacial decomposition
of Carolinian forest floors,
the certainty that we must
all blend into the ground.
It is rot without rebirth.

The Hurons have moved on
but the mission that promised
them salvation remains.
It sits in the unfamiliar calm
that followed the firedance.
A stalwart calm that lingers
beneath the spires and turrets
that slide at wide unbalanced angles
like a skin trying to shed itself.

Gulls Flood the Sky at Point de Montreal

Upon arrival, it should be noted,
that we too ran with outstretched
arms through the land cleared back
from the river and sent the gulls,
thick like whitecaps on a tempest
lake, into the place the creator
meant for them. It was our way
of claiming a first memory of land
left to the survivors of wars
and the calamities of migration.

Gulls, panicked screams into grey
drizzle of sky, scattered back over
water, clear across a border measured
by paper maps and tax collectors
in border guard blue. Their retreat
becomes our welcome to this mission
of divisions, the sense being
that this naked point of earth
along the quick moving straits,
where our present rides against
the currents between lakes,
is borrowed like chattel taken
from those like us here,
arms outstretched, chin skyward
in a wide-open grassy field.

Moravian 47

There was a time before numbers like these.
Where the wallpaper of a two-story farmhouse
was collaged together out of yellowed Toronto
Star and Detroit News pages and a boy could
lay back on a grandparent's bed daydreaming
about Woodward Ave at rush hour or Bay St
at night. Because the busiest days in this corner
of Kent County were treaty days and the worst
sin was sitting out in the sun too long
because then you couldn't look like
the daydreamed masses of pale-faced people
that crowded what was Woodward and shopped
at Epps and Tepperman's for fifty dollar suits.

And all of this he relays to me
in a simple motion of his left hand
through the car window as we pass
a stand of oak and ash. He says "That was
my grandparent's place." Moravian 47
becomes good ole Bucktown
as we swing towards the community centre
and pass the youngest cousins Peters
potlaching a brown bag
of white man's burden
walking proudly along the middle
of the rough paved road.

Myths of Dark Waters as Seen from Atop the Conservation Drive Overpass

Beliefs begin with the view of fireworks,
distant celebrations of the tenure of empires,
amidst stopped traffic and AM transmissions
refracted through treetops. Beneath the skin
of this city moves a smattering of headlights,
moving like smelt through shallow dark waters.

Five miles from the river myths of dark water,
how colour and scene of detonating fireworks
drowns our past, whitewashes it like headlights
into darkened tall-grass prairies, and empires
become clever ways to build history. Brown skin
is a secondary sin, corrected by Jesuit missions.

Between gunpowder thuds, that sweet mission
voice of Aretha pounds gospel into dark water
that would burn but for this humid June, skin
wrapped in creeping sweat and constant firework
slaps to remind of leather and metal blows empires
used to straighten roads through forests. Headlights

burning through the lanes behind us. Headlights
churn up a new path of souls for the missions'
orphaned charges, freeways the one true empire's
ways. Coureurs de Bois knew that dark water
was best not stirred and collapse comes as fireworks
spread like middle-thunder at dawn. Light kisses skin

as another car pulls onto the freeway shoulder, skin
and sense pulled from shadow by headlights.
Ascending and falling in quickening pace, fireworks

illuminate in kaleidoscope the others gathered, mission prayers given up to awe in moments when dark waters could reflect oil slick copies of what makes our empires.

Reflections blur in waters' constant motion, empires turned to ribbons of neon light as if sweat-soaked skin bled a Patrick Swayze movie. Beneath, these dark waters are as impermeable as Canada Shield. Headlights pulling away from the shoulder as if those missions again left us in silence to witness those distant fireworks.

The crescendo of fireworks does not craft empires nor return those shuttered missions. Doubtless, your skin is warmed by headlights as they cut night like dark water.

Dancer in Front of the Thistle Club

Beneath the small lip overhang
of the Thistle Club, the young girl,
mid-western chubby, bounces through
slide steps of Bonnie Dundee.
The thrum of traffic passing, distant
grumble of bagpipes, gives way
to the remembered urgency
of a fiddle, the shuffle
of cloth lined feet, and the bob
of pinned up curls.

Ecru skin turns flush
by the slow push of humid summer
air. The descent of sun brings no relief.

Straight backed
twist, chin up,
and hold.

She moves generations
with each pounce.
Muscles commensurate
in the pull and release
of her mother's
or aunt's in those summers
before the life
they too inherited.

Blue and white tartan legs whirl
through steps and reels, she pushes
and pulls her feet along concrete and stops

again. With a flutter of curls
and slumped teenage posture she darts
through the club's door.
Old men laugh like spring geese
and are cut short
with the closing
of the club's door.

In the Twilight of the Reign of the Nain Rouge

On those fall nights
declared for the devil
we didn't know, in awe
we would stand
along the riverfront
and watch as a city
would tear itself open
and into the air above.

A river's width separating
tragedy from art form
and it burned so quietly
and not so far from us.
Sirens, small like Christmas
lights on seasonal mall displays
were distant, to be watched
never touched. This world was
cut in two by a river. Our side
the one with this view,
that side the one burning
itself into the night
we shared. Each fire a halo
that brought with it
memories of humid nights,
refracting yellow street posts,
and AM radio crackle in the close
of another American Century.

The hope that maybe this year
the halos and the sirens
would push that red demon
back to its river bottom home

and the slow burning tragedy
of the city on the other side
of the medicine line could
finally fizzle out like white hot
coals thrown to the fast currents
of the river that separates us.

Mason 20

We had dreamed of this before
the short drive across the border
to find those mythic American women,
wholesome and impossibly beautiful
like trade videos promoting conferences
and the straight box growth in Detroit's
McNamara days.

We pass though rubble-
heavy concrete overpasses, moving
as fast as that K-car would allow us.
On the lamb from our hinterland home
we chant road signs like mantras
on the path to enlightenment.

Breaking west from Taylor
it rains hard and fast as we pass
Detroit Metro, airbuses scrape
highway light posts and we pass
signs for cities that come to us,
well-matched songs from Zeppelin
to Seger to Grand Funk Railroad.
Going to Chicago and the radio
burns like it too had sold its soul
to that riff burning devil at the Delta Forks.

None of this worries us.

Because in that farm town in the middle

of this mitten of a state, there are women
with long-black-wavy hair and a posture
like nothing we've seen amongst the French,

British, and Polish gals of that place we call
home. So, we ply northward from Jackson,
the three of us acting like a Jack Kerouac novel
unrolling in 9mm camera clarity before our eyes,
knowing that only pure speed and energy
could cut the lines we've come through
and lead us to the promise of soft American flesh.

Returning Home to Detroit UHF

We returned to a summer heated attic
and a song from Final Fantasy. Run out
like two dogs after a short walk round
the traffic circle and back now. Tired.
Hungry. The old black and white TV
was on UHF 56 from midtown Detroit
and the colors were still all 1970s
afro-pride and oranges and yellows
and those fully leaded Chryslers,
Plymouths, and soft topped Buicks.

All that promise held at the end
of our late night trip to Mac's Milk
for beef jerky, near beer, and glimpses of
older more street savvy public school girls.

And he had been playing the whole time,
the three dime jingle of 8-bit anime repeated
like a Dickie Dee through tree-lined Walkerville.
Pressed finger cursing of a game that neither of us
could understand beyond the short dress
cartoon princess and great pastel explosions
that shook demons from a two dimensional world.
All of that world at war was in the foreground
of a 50s space alien film with Leslie Neilson that
couldn't take us from our oh-so-worldly desires.

In the glow of twin TVs, we had to figure
that his 8-bit girls were all the more real
than our corner store popsicle girls.
Atop the house on Devonshire court
heat never dissipated into the night
and we would all fall to sleep

between the bubblegum chorus of Queen
and the overplayed screams of long aged
actresses. And we might sleep through
a replay of those rib shack commercials
And he, he would play through to dawn,
maybe well past it, and always insist
that after just one more level, we could
all go out and find out what all the UHF
noise was really going on about.

Uptick

Was it the uptick
that made you sure
finger snaps connected
on that Eddie Rabbit
track? The one
that reminded me
of stop lights
reflected off
the sheen of Tecumseh road
asphalt at the end
of a June thunderstorm.

Best put
as the training season
marked by,
as it must be,
an abundance
of precipitation,
cool nights
and the neon glow
of Most Precious Blood
reminding drivers
of Sunday morning redemptions.

It's all uptick though,
all Black's Photo shop,
and the yellow and brown benches
of a Brian Mulroney Tim Horton's,
all poppy optimism
in the face of deluges
and stretched wool clouds.

But it too
is dark
in the manner that things
that matter most
move in
and feel safest.

It had to be
that all-so-sure-of-itself
finger pop that rang out
for a quarter measure,
it was sugar pop
Eddie Rabbit
with the UHF
late night beard
and his dirty south
hair falling freely
behind his upturned collar.

It was that uptick.
That was the one
you understood
and left me with,
thinking about
those rainstorms
and the way
redemption comes
with sunrise
and the slow fade-out
on a track too full of love
to simply stop on its own.

Reminiscing about Hoffa
at the Ivy Rose Motor Inn

On the upper catwalk, above the radiating black top of the
    parking lot below,
an orange sun slips beneath slow bursts of cloud and is framed
    by paint caked railings.
I watch over fifties, maybe forties, peach walls and patched tar
    roofs, watch as they
give way to the steady sprawl of city as it pushes away from
    the river at an even horizon.
Across the strip mall and smoke stack expanse, Jimmy Hoffa
    vanished thirty-five years ago
beneath similar skies. Skies that now build towards a bluish,
    whitish, pinkish crescendo.

Blurred lines of cars move past carrion splattered curbs and
    skim rust stained sidewalks.
Sidewalks left empty in the growth of night and the
    approaching curtains of rain.
The junkyard next door billows smoke the color of bruises,
    threatening
in steady upward thrusts in advance of approaching rain. Rain
    that could separate
metal from air and wash the carrion clean away. The air
    around me holds a metallic bite
of consumed car parts, the odor of an imminent storm held at
    a river's distance.

In a room below, the rattle of bottles becomes muffled voices
less hushed, somewhat violent in their embrace of the
    darkness of leased space.
The earth itself fumbles for climax, sparked by distant
    lightning, held off
by the smoke stack beside me. The concrete of the walkway

below me is thinner
than scraped tile and rattles in the bluster of distant surging
thunder, rolls
with the collapse of a Taurus trunk and the plaintiff honk of a
nearby car alarm.

Hoffa was the union man in a city that carried home with it
the afterbirth
of Union Hall cigarette smoke and bootleg liquor. Always the
rumors of darker things,
the silent movement of money and discreteness of freshly
disturbed dirt lingered.
The empty lot of the Red Fox those decades ago never
changed those facts
for men and women that once had reason to come home
happy/tired at night.

Once great sounds of civilization turn to animal moaning
below.
And thunderheads keep growing in the backlight of sunset
and
slink away towards the deliverance of others. Their sun kissed
sins
alone in this aging riverside city have been tempted again
by the cleansing act of rain against the hard packed summer
earth.

The Arms of Christ Reveal Depths
of Grey at the Edge of Ford City

Palms extended skyward and framed
the downriver edge of Belle Isle.
Rusted fences stationed between,
Christ stands before loading docks,
long empty, blue waters beyond.

Behind him, the edge of Ford City
with its drive-shaft straight seigneurie
turned to that appropriate hue
of grey and dust that follows
factory work, unions, and things
not promised by soviet trade unions
and the post empire grit of boreal forest
as they play catch-up with industrial
clear-cuts. The rumble of freighters,
diesel clouds trailing to Lake St.Clair,
cannot shake those skyward palms
nor unsettle the loosest of grit.

Turtle island dug up and passed out
to sea before these outstretched arms
and the twin, rust dripping bell towers
of Holy Rosary Church. All of it blessed
by shift work that ended in Habs' games
on flickering bar-top televisions
and the kind of personal oblivion
that follows twelve hour shifts,
quarter-hour delivered pints of OV
and the raw want of avoiding
the disappointments of home.

Outside, the grey spreads from curb
to curb to sky, back to barstool, brought
like it must be, from the old country
to this country and stamped-out
for passers-by, locals, and the lost.
Witness industrial life blood turned
to nubs of ash from rained out fire dancers.

All of it, unfurled beneath the steps
leading to Christ, his outstretched arms,
bearded chin upturned to unending sun
and the great patient acceptance
to the way that bit by bit the land
leaves and the newcomers stay
in these depths of grey that hang
all too tightly to Old Ford City.

Before the Approaching Front

The feel of tires grinding back,
against the pockmarked pavement,
resonates as you move past corrugated
doors of this factory that stretches on
like proletariat warfare, girdling blocks
and blocks of worker housing. Night,
electric and lazy with summer
puddling up against August emerges
only at the edges of its distant stacks.

Road grinds back and you feel it slow
as the empty street meets red reflected,
until there is only windshield wipers
and the muffled chorus of Night Ranger.
The storm front flashes its presence
as it comes in over the distant river,
middle thunder giving way to clay white
bursts of a tempest ear-marked to rattle
tree limbs, traffic lights, and window panes

Near Gate Three, at the quarter mark
of the night shift, three pot-bellied, loose-
t-shirt men emerge from the fence. Sober,
like you never were, and they fumble
with cellphones and lit cigarettes,
throwing heaters and all too heavy smoke
into the rumbling sky. Supplicants,

their prayers to the effect that there must be
more than this endless building. Waiting,
all of them for a call or text or simply
quiet, just enough so that their ringing ears

could stop, maybe to shout their quotidian
concerns into the night's charged atmosphere.

It is met with the groan of wiper blades
while an empty street meets red light
reflected and more rain holds back
behind the front, those men are the only
evidence you'll get that shift-change
doesn't create men from car parts.
Theirs is a world that you pass by
in the shadow of another summer storm,
their struggles, pasts, and futures
held tight to them like bolts gunned
into liftgates and rocker panels as that line
marches by in clean Four Tops rhythm.

Even made in the dark, money and men
must come to face the approaching storm.
But for you, red switches over to green
and the road growls back at you as you
make your way north towards that front.

Rains come as Blessings at Brighton Beach

To hell with the way rain falls
into this mostly empty part of the city.
Steady and drenching from above,
emerging from the shelf of low-
lying clouds and dulled down city
lights. These bonfires of pallets
and empty beer cases burn on,
and the way that far too mature
and jig sawed trees hold the light in,
lets you know this place is of itself
and itself alone. Brighton Beach

and us locals lost in a backwoods
ritual want to hear Toto, in spite of
this death metal garage band, quarts
of Labbatt Fifty, plastic cups of gut rot,
and the ever-falling rain hitting out-
stretched tarps. We are akin to starlings

to these transient drug runners. They shake
us and all of our chants off; passing
more fuel on to their one-night fires,
and raging on the way roman candles
burn into the fickle post-industrial night.
And we, like wild dogs cry out against

all of it, knowing no one has stuck
to this land since the Mohawks dispersed
the Wyandot and the blessed rains
washed the Beaver Wars from thin topsoil.

There's nothing that a hundred men
or the group of us could do but cry
like dogs into this, the blessed,
blessed rainy night where the straits
become the wide open Erie shallows.

Stirrings of Things Buried Along the Shores of Sandwich

Against the shore
the hushed pater of squirrels
before sunset
gives way to hissing
as Ford Steel releases
smelter heat,
sizzling into the hyacinthine
of midnight where Sandwich
meets the straits
and the city lights
disperse into the murk
nearest the water line.

Across the strait,
steam clouds enshroud
industrial stacks that reveal
the rhythmic flashing
of white and red beacons,
warnings to low-flying aircraft,
reminders of shore to
freighters passing in the night.
This is the empty place

where men come
to make money
and burn the past
into a vapour
that dissipates
into night air.

Steam trails off like a veil
cascading into oil-slick eddies
just below the opposite bank.

Here, above
the nearby shore,
where once dancers shook
fire and bones
while hide-covered feet
pounded awake an earth
soothed to slumber
by the downgrade rush
of water to the great ancestral lands.

Tonight the falling miasma,
the persistent beacons,
silent in their domination
of everything
is punctuated
by the distant
clanging of metal.

All of it burning on
in this late autumn night.
Every last bit trying
but failing to erase
the murmur of waves lapping
steadily against the shore.

Cargo Arrives at YQG

We watch them land
these night line cargo planes
coming in low over Walker.
They are all black shadow,
punctuated by possibilities
of white metal and the red
white red beacons.

From the front seat
they should be more
and we know it.

It is the first hour
of late night AM radio
the question of Red Cloud
is brought up; what
would he have said
about cargo planes
landing at night?

But our ancestors
have been left as villains
and villains have no thoughts
on things such as auto-part
shipments, logistics,
and the plight of two
Delaware boys, waiting
out sunrise in a Ford
hatchback in the lot
of a Petro-Canada.

Through the Cicada Summer

During this cicada summer,
we crawl along the parkway
cutting toward Windsor,
within constant eyeshot
of the opening straits.
Inland, the river constricts,
slows, and spills into marsh.

In full view the rough edges
of the Medicine Line
as land's end foliage cuts
borders and is punctuated
by provincial road signs
and the scraggly ground
of unmarked roadways.
Gulls, forever in warfare,
circle the marsh's edge
then move inland,
together in distant pairs.

Follow as we must
against the gentle slope
that drains rainwater
to sweet water seas,
we follow the road inland.
Behind us, that asphalt bridge
vanishes in the slow curves
of River Canard and unsteady waves
of cattails rolling in the wind.

Between these shores,
two hundred years before,
prophets pushed back

against the forgotten war front,
holding the line
of now extinct sovereign land,
the belief that survival
trumps history and who we are
is measured by the ways
we resist things we were.

Saint Joseph's turrets rise
white tipped like sentinels
above the river's slow drip.
Stretched heavenward they grasp
at passing clouds, open hands
outstretched to draw sky
to earth. Yet, River Canard
moves on thick with lilies
and slow like migrating honey.
Bunched in tight formations,
pushing into the heart of the land,
the lilies waltz against cattails
and fallen branches, skimming
the river's surface in a slow dance
becoming of a cicada summer.

Kicking up Cattails with Crazy Horse on the Queen's Highway

What could you say of cattails
swaying in a ditch between you
and a tobacco field that can't be
heard in passing traffic and mumble
of Neil Young's Harvest Moon
through a sun melted tape deck.
Those urgent punches of wind
and heat and noise that come
like clouds of gnats, patchy
and free from a four-four rhythm.
They might rattle cattails like wind
chimes, fleshy in a lakeside breeze.
Underneath, Crazy Horse could be
ditch bottom kicking at the roots
of that glorious gutter weed because
red-wing blackbirds have tendencies
to remind us who should be
sovereign of this land.

Waiting along a Queen's highway
thirty minutes outside of Tilbury,
your Honda's radiator blowing fog
clouds like fall mornings alongside
a Kawartha lake. Words fail
in the same way that the word
Muskoka cannot translate urbane
highway life into Group of Seven
Canada. You think about canoes,
and herons, and that decidedly
isolated feeling that every single
Canadian pulls from that loon call
lying behind every Neil vocal line.

And when your buddy arrives at
your ditch-side cabin by the reeds
you ignore the coolant's sugary burn
and turn up "Down by the River."
The trickle of heavy picked guitar
pushes the cattails into a lean
away from traffic that could chase
off those surly blackbirds
and for a country minute
the highway is empty
and wide
and as silent
as the wind
must let it
be.

Inland from the Shores of Erie

Then there was that time
you hauled a yellow catfish
from the creek bottom on line
that was far from proper test.
Halfway between break rocks
and the overpass we had drifted
inland from a tight rope walk
along the shores of Erie.

Yellow like the pale fire
of desiccate grass lines that run
along the road side from here
to Wheatley
to Lakeshore
to sweet sweet lips
of Rondeau Bay.

Maybe because our part
of the second largest country
on the globe holds the same
light to the things that power us
through harsh winters we hardly
know, maybe because no living
creature should be that sickly
of a colour, or maybe we always
believed the essence of all things
is through the freedom they live,
no matter the baby-shit mud
that colours their sky.

You let that catfish free.

It slipped beneath the slow rolling
ripples that proved this creek
was part earth part water
and our canoe drifted surely
towards the shade
of the nearby overpass.

Deliberate Motions at 30,000 Feet

We came to the boardwalk
through tight-walled cottages
that blocked the road from the lake.
We came to the park because our city
and its bled over brown sky was too damned
much for another heavy June morning.
Where wooden boards met the edges
of cattail forests, the marsh bottom boiled
with the pregnant fin tops of carp.
And you said that the way they writhed
reminded you of the North Atlantic as you
looked on from a cruising altitude of 30,000 feet.
Except that our view was cloudless, expansive
before us and less deliberate than the movement
of currents between landmasses.

As the humidity peaked upward
and sunbeams slipped though the cattails
to slick up the fat backs of carp,
I jingled my car keys like a diner bell,
out of habit. Unseen nearby, a red-winged
blackbird trilled. And you glared at me
like an unsteady landing at Pearson
while the fins and backs pushed harder
against each other and small swells
of marsh water pushed at the boardwalk.

You, returned from the other continent,
couldn't smile back or think of the blackbird
because all that was part of the reasons you
left all this behind. And as I returned the keys
to my pocket and shrugged off any clash
of our two worlds, we both looked up at the halo
as the sun pushed through over hazy Lake Erie.

Sharing Daydreams at Historical Site 41

She showed us the gravel pit
that used to be the latrine
when this part of Upper Canada
was the type of place you would
send a river man on the lam.
And she smiled like she knew
that there was no way an empire
would let a women into a red coat,
celebrating the victories that only time
can bear out. Adjusting the black hat
with its government restored white
pom-pom at its two-foot summit,
her smile widened like this was the best
part of dressing up; the part where
you share your imagination, tell
complete strangers what you can
daydream of when no-one is around.
When I ask if she has rolled down
the hills that used to make up the town
walls, she tells me that's where the latrine
emptied out. Her voice deceptive,
as if she knows that we all do things
that others consider gross or wrong,
reminds us that this is a historical site,
the kind of place where anthropologists
come down from London on weekday
mornings and play Columbus all over again.

Following Junior Hockey through Kent County

The names, you said,
of places like Kent County
were the ones
you remembered most
of the time
before you came here.

Lying down, the light
of passing interchanges
and reflective signs
were lures under water
and the stars
as they hovered above
the 401 were still,
like cattails before the rain.

We were past the lights
of West Lorne, maybe
closing in on Ridgetown
or Blenheim when I realized
you, half asleep, were sing-songing
those names like your parents had
in a Balkland apartment.

Through the chipped
hatchback window
we were backwards
to a musty carpet
that demarked
the ribbon of land
we now shared.

I wanted to imagine
the white noise
of bald tires at 90 kmph

to be the warm
hum of planets
as they spun
brightly around stars,
deciding lifelines
and every sound
we will know.

The push of wind
on the metal of that car
was the rocking
of a canoe on Lake St. Clair,
a breeze through ash trees,
the embrace of this,
our southern Canadian homeland.

As you murmured
some Serbian words
that I couldn't understand,
but found beautiful
in the exotic and unsteady melody
as they left with your breath
and warmed a winter night,
I couldn't help but wonder
if there was a war
that still drove you
to the sounds of the places
that flung by us
in the hiss of tires and asphalt.
Or if the rattle of pucks
around the end boards
and the want of warmth
in a junior hockey rink
were unsteady and exotic enough
to drive away the reasons
to speak unrepeatable sounds.

And the Word Grows Older
than the People

It cuts, this green hue
of broad, bent-over leaves,
lacerates the damp air
below red-sided smoke houses.

With heaven pulled close
and bathed in grey
this atavistic ritual smudge
stands empty, alone,
too far cleansed.

This Kent County roadside pull-out opens
into mist of four-hundred-year-old longing.
Petun, the ancienne sounds for tobacco
and the people wiped away by children
of settlers and the wars to cleanse
the remainders,
feels heavy when spoken.

Perhaps Tionantite,
among the first names spoken
to the ancestors of these leaves,
first planted by people outlived
by both plant and name.

And in this landscape
heavy in the silence of a place lost
by those that named it,
I mumble the syllables
of the name Wyandot.
Against this humidity

they come weak
and dissipate
like a final breath
before leaving.

In that low-strung grey mist
of the early summer bath
of front-driven rain,
witness atop the peak
of the furthest smoke house
from the road,
a red-tailed hawk surveying
the dilated rows
of mature tobacco.

Stern, breast to the mist,
he watches for movement
then flies south
towards the lake
and into the even-grey body
of a sky
pushed too low.

Ice Break-Up Arrives From Sarnia

Our winter continues to disintegrate,
and I watch as in steady stride debris
from its high distant suns and coarse
biting winds, they pass the park's edge.
Barren trees hold back a sinking sky
with countless out-stretched spindles
of last season's growth. Feel the sun
warming against the wind's bite
and the better sense to not stand
here alone on a closed beach
in the wrong season for exposure.
Hope arrives even in discomfort.

That broad shallow diminutive kettle
of a lake, now named for our patron
saint of television, ferries last winter's
coldest sweet water chunks past us.
We shall arise from this white-capped
twilight and the hard light of car
traffic migrating between warmth
and ominous cold of county lines.
Our discomfort lies in familiarity

with the names we haven't given things.
As each shelf of ice runs past, realization
comes like prophecy that surely we must
return to this place on this beach
and the dirt grey slush of winter
will give way to fresh tender sprouts
and naked flesh. In the end, currents
and subtle movements of sky force
every hard winter down the rivers
towards the oceans that brought
the most unwelcomed evils upon us
and free us from all too familiar cold.

The Stonefish Boys Bring Little Medicine to the Doorsteps of Ontario

The Stonefish boys worked big medicine along the banks of the Thames. They worked it outwards, away from the patchwork tobacco farms, past the spectred lines of lost reservations. Medicine carved into the folds of chiseled wood, displayed in red ochre water paints and brilliant shellac.

The Stonefish boys became big medicine along the banks of the Thames. They carved wood with it, shaped tree stumps into the Indians that the Upper Canada outside of Bucktown had always wanted them to be; picturesque, chiseled like Grey Owl, unrelenting in their working lives, quiet in protest. Big medicine worked the Stonefish boys into the twins of craft and heritage: the craft of building dime-store wooden Indians, the heritage of accepting the chiseled wooden lines as fleshy form. Theirs was a heritage and craft to be shared, brought to Ontario's doorsteps by mail order.

Big medicine manifested itself in different ways. Each brother was best with certain skills; shading wooden skin with red ochre, chiseled feathers appearing flexible in neon light, surveyor line tautness of stoic mouths forever on the verge of speaking. A silent defiance that followed each viewer.

Their dime-store wooden Indians became little medicine in the hands of those that bought them. Owning creations of what passed through Stonefish hands reminded those around them about what heritage can be claimed by buying craftsmanship from those left in the wake of land settlements.

This Stonefish little medicine greets the world as if it were freshly burnt sweetgrass and sage,
without the trauma of passing the sacred through generations.

They stand where Indians once did, minor medicine beside
Petro-Canada gas pumps, highway exit Tim Hortons, and
knick-knack shops.

Bathed in technicolor, the Stonefish boys bring forth
word of their medicine during twenty minute ad spots on
afterhours "info" television. The Stonefish boys accept four
easy payments of $79.95. No C.O.Ds, P.O. Boxes, and
No reservation addresses accepted. International orders are
welcome.

The Eagles Bought their Weed
from Walpole Island

Urban Indian heritage begins
with one of those nights,
that wood door, Walkerville
row house charming, spinning
on its sky blue backdrop,
sacred turquoise at the centre
of that hand-me down vinyl,
turned at a clean 45 rpm,
Henley moving from groove
to needle to high-fidelity speakers.

Around you, punctuated by euchre,
laughter, and Leo Racicot ads
play back at you. Punchlines
emerging from an Emerson set
that arose ten Easters ago,
all of it making the simple act
of getting by unfold into ceremony,
the Eagles playing welcome drum
to this gathering of the nations,
one greatest hit after another.

In between the dark
and the light that vinyl rolls
and Henley harmonizes
in the perfect seventies'
peel of blue collar trans-genre
twang. For five whole verses
we are sure as hell they bought
their weed from the Walpole boys
that everyone of us knows
on a first name basis. Because if

a Delaware guy, living in a lakeside
town his ancestors sold-off
for a few dozen hectares
of tobacco land along the Thames,
if he could feel the bottomless pit
of longing these guys laid down
on vinyl, the belief follows
that they must have been cleansed
with same smudge we used
before our newfound ceremony.

We know that without land
we are no more than collections
of ceremonies borrowed
from the habits and chattel
we carry with us to the home
we construct along the way.

Crows Return to the Banks of the Thames

So it happens each autumn
the trees shall grow black
and perhaps groan under
the combined weight of migration.
And each crow perched above
the slow cut of the river, narrow,
rocky, shallow, recalls that sound.
And mimes it back and sings
of time, all against the pantheon
grey above the flats between lakes.

Memory, bound to feather
and cartilage carries etchings
of previous migrations
and brings them to winter here.
The thought follows that
where we winter is home,
the places we haunt
are recorded in our very being.

On these river banks that too
host refuges of the wrong side
of the Medicine line, them too
saddled with unfulfilled
loyalist promises, discount
gas and tax-free smokes,
murders announce themselves
and make evening news
segments around the Dominion.
As before the arrival of fronts,
garbage bins are disturbed
and the cooling air is hard
in the knowledge that all we work

for can be turned out with as much
as a Kodachrome of our childhood,
a knowing that jars the locals enough
to slip out into the cold. Fireworks,
pots and pans, plaintiff bleats
of car horns heard through branches
and the rustle of wings as the push
comes to keep the longest residents
migrating and silence their

blatant hungry calls that echo
into the Kent County night.

Kings Highway 18 Cuts towards
Antediluvian Fires

From the mid-point
of the moraine it is
unmistakable.
This first highway
folds against them
into the blue rim
of horizon, now hours past
moonrise, still orange,
burning gentle light
like evening storms
departing.

Unmistakable glow cast
from the slow alchemy
turning prairie and forest
into that turtle-shell city,
stretches out above
where road and horizon meet.

Standing in this quiet,
punctuated briefly
by shaking leaves
in the upper branches
and the rustle of soybeans
in the occasional
lake-drawn winds,
night is ripped open,
by passing cars,
cold soil upturned
to lingering heat
of the day past,

torn straight out
towards the orange glow
by passing cars.

And they are moving,
in the way that clouds do
after fronts blow clear,
lazy like fireflies,
lingering as they fade,
distant grind of tires
against cooling asphalt,
they gouge the surface
as they leave.

And the third car
in the last minute
speeds past,
heading north-westward
towards that electric light
at the edge of the Medicine Line.

It was said
when Tecumseh lost
the new homeland
along the Wabash
that comets couldn't lie
until the ground shook
and the front moved north.
Harrison's men burned
the forests to chase away
the Indigenous night.
From as far away as Wheatley
the horizon burned
an angry, fearful citrus orange.

From Colchester south
to the old Anderdon land,
before vineyards
and spider removal signs,
the western horizon
burned with frontier wars
and paths men cut inland.

The diminishing taillights
grow frantic red
as they disappear
into the darkness
that nightfall brings
to farmland, concessions,
and the very things
that cause so many
to come here,
fleeing the fire
that hides
the night sky
from an encroaching
darkness.

Pond Hockey in Middlesex

But what of the sound
of a puck as it rattles
with cold earth thuds
along and around the end
boards? You between
blue line and hash marks,
stick pulled in against your
waist and that puck's sound
cuts jagged-edge through wind
gusts from a half-frozen lake.

Does it match the trill
of a red-winged blackbird
balancing atop a snowcapped
cattail? You, beneath that
fresh paint swipe of blue sky
and along the smudged white end
boards, does that rattle
of granite solid rubber
as it slings against splintered
wood remind you of hot chocolate
and goal horns, the excitement
of doubleheaders first from Winnipeg
the second from Calgary?

Or the way your old man flipped
off Ulf Samuelson from the sofa
because we had to find enemies
we could recognize from afar.
It was the same way you looked
at every other player on that pond
because survival is a family trait
and that thick rolling sound was

like the first notes of a Lightfoot
tune, a beacon into the cold dark
of a January Bucktown Saturday night,
follow it and it shall light your path.

Does it remind you of the stern
and motherly gaze of the Queen
as she looked down from the rafters
of Winnipeg Arena in that first game?
Do you hear in its certain slowing
the knowledge that treaties are rules
and cockeyed refs are politicians
playing favourites with the life blood
of every Saturday night on every bit
of remaining land? Our portrait Queen,
as distant as she is stern, presides over
each game before the great relocation.

But this, this is a simple pick-up game
of pond hockey, in mid-afternoon
away from the lights and national
anthem bravado. No Bob Cole cawing
into the broad forgetful night, only
the all too low sun in a far too young
afternoon on an ice pond
near the north shore of Erie.

Another Blenheim Saturday Night

Maybe it was the manner in which
the ashtray landed in the street,
with the crash of a thousand
ceramic shards collapsing to asphalt,
perhaps it was the vibrant orange
of that country girl's *whazzup* hat
that made you think of retirement homes
and the threat of unscripted sponge baths.

Blenheim in its sodium vapour
lamp splendour rings into the night
like farm hands on the lam from the boss.
Here we try and sneak through the clouds
of just another night after the louder
memories and what remains is the thought
that without Treaty 2 none of these intersections
could meet at any angle, at any place.

That reclaimed vintage and now pulverized
ashtray and the not so near miss getting
with the only hot white girl in Kent County
on that night, we know none of these crimes
could be counted. Five men, two treatied,
set loose against a town that so few
remember because the highway comes
only so close and every injustice is best
left to Phds while the rest of us
muddle on towards things like sovereignty
and small battles we believe we have
left to reclaim what signatures on paper
can wrestle from the essence of people.

Burning Wild Turkey at Rondeau Beach

The sand of Lake Erie burned
with a poured slick of wild turkey, lit
by the triangled end of your clove cigarette.
And beyond the middle row of breakers
half grown men leapt from submerged
picnic tables. A storm out past Long Point
forced the lake up against the beach line.
And they crash into the surf proclaiming
with each jackknife splash that Bonzo never died
and this young world belonged solely to them.

We cheered on those men of ours
that were willing to battle
the chest high waves, and lash back
at the cast-offs of that distant storm.
Our backs to the thicket of Carolinian
forest and the flat gravel campground
it was built around, we cheered them on
with the heater of that last cigarette.
And we both agreed that Presence
wasn't as bad an album as we had once
believed.

And the turkey burned dimly against
the urgency of distant and trailing lightning.
Burned against the absence of rain.
Burned and lit the edges of cool sand blue.
We laughed because we were beyond
the drunkenness of that vile booze, laughed
because we felt some of us were beating
back the lines of the storm. You and I shared
the dense spice of the same cigarette.

But we didn't lose our shirts,
or swim out to those submerged tables.
We dug our feet into the sand
and tried to imagine the delicacy
of our friends' battles; Their dance and dives
and yells at a storm as it retreated north
following the edge of the lake.

Between the rolling surf,
I heard you hum the refrain from
"Fool in the Rain" as you handed me
the last nub of cigarette
and the lines of flame fell
into the blue sand shadows
above our feet.

Truly the Manitou were Active and Kindly

This thought occurs late,
sun setting behind the Ren Cen
painting the sky salmon flesh
with streaks of long past jetliners.
The river swells with the early waves
of storms crawling in across the plains.

And follows itself with calm,
as in those little sleeps
between bouts of restlessness;
like the black-haired girl who smiled
white as sun kissed bones and proud
at the Bucktown Pow-Wow last fall,
before running playfully off
to the gravel parking lot.

By the ancient sturgeon pools
alongside the abandoned pump house
there are ripples and waves
on the calm river surface.
The motion is that of a world
once born on the turtle's back
as it looks for another footing
upon which to rest
its kind and very active self.

Acknowledgements

The author would like to thank the Ontario Arts Council and the Canada Council for the Arts for their generous support in helping to bring this work to fruition. Many thanks to Catherine Bowman, Maura Stanton, Tony Ardizzone, and Don Belton for their tutelage and patience. Special thanks to the many lit mags, editors, and readers that over the years have shown kindness to my work. The following poems from this collection have appeared in the listed journals below.

"Barometric Pressure" *Contemporary Verse 2*
"Myths of Dark Water as Seen From Atop the Conservation Drive Overpass" *Contemporary Verse 2*
"Coming to the Mission of the Hurons" Paradigm Journal
"Burning Wild Turkey" *Construction Magazine*
"Reminiscing about Hoffa at the Ivy Rose Motor Inn" *COE Review*
"Through the Cicada Summer" as an earlier draft appeared as "Lilies of River Canard" in *San Pedro River Review*
"Mason 20" *Reed Magazine*

About the Author

D.A. Lockhart lives in Windsor, ON. He holds a MFA in Creative Writing from Indiana University where he held a Neal-Marshall Fellowship in Fiction. He has received numerous grants from the Ontario Arts Council and Canada Council for the Arts for both his poetry and his fiction. His work has appeared throughout North America in journals such as *Vinyl, Contemporary Verse 2, the Windsor Review, the Mackinaw,* and the *Sugar House Review.* He is a member of the Moravian of the Thames First Nation.